D1201814

The Work of Our Hands

The Work of Our Hands

The Art of Martin Erspamer, OSB

OCP Christmas 2007

MERSPAMER OSB

Foreword by

Archabbot Justin DuVall, OSB

Preface by

Guerric DeBona, OSB

Edition 20368
ISBN-13: 978-1-56929-078-1

The Work of Our Hands: The Art of Martin Erspamer, OSB

An imprint of OCP
5536 NE Hassalo
Portland, OR 97213-3638

Phone: 1-800-LITURGY (548-8749)
E-mail: liturgy@ocp.org
Web: ocp.org and pastoralpress.com
Printed in Mexico

Publisher: John J. Limb
Director of Editorial Processes: Eric Schumock
Director of Artist Relations & Product Development: Thomas Tomaszek
Project Editor: Bari Colombari
Editing Assistance: Mónica Rodríguez
Book Layout: Susan Irish
Project and Art Direction: Jean Germano
Dust Cover Art by Martin Erspamer, OSB. Top center panel of the Saint Meinrad Shrine in the Archabbey Church of Our Lady of Einsiedeln, St. Meinrad, Indiana.
Cover photo, pp. 21, 81, 89 by John Farless.

RRD-RM 09/07

TABLE OF CONTENTS

Introduction

Brother Martin is as simple and as complex as the art he creates. When you first see his line drawings, they appear simplistic; further examination reveals each mark is made to convey rich symbolism. Like medieval art, created as a sacred script, each piece is designed for contemplation.

It is difficult to remember when I first saw Brother Martin's art, but I remember the feeling I was left with. I knew at once that what I was looking at was created by someone with a strong knowledge of art and a deep understanding of theology. (At that time he was Brother Steve Erspamer, SM.) I was working as the art director for OCP and searching for images appropriate for use in our publications. I spoke with Martin several times by phone, always when pots were clanging and he was making dinner for himself or his beloved Airedale Hampton. Eventually we met at a Form and Reform conference sometime in the early 90s. Our working relationship turned into a friendship that I value to this day.

Brother Martin was born in Iron Mountain, Michigan, and attended Central Catholic Marianist High School in San Antonio, Texas. As a child he was not drawn to the mystery of the liturgy, nor was he that taken by Mass. It was his Latin teacher, a young Marianist brother, who planted a seed by asking him if he had ever thought about being a brother. The idea stayed with him, and by his seventeenth birthday he decided to enter the Society of Mary. His first year was spent in the Marianist Scholasticate in San Antonio, and it was there that art and faith came together.

He did his novitiate in Galesville, Wisconsin, and took his vows there. He worked in the Marianist art studios in St. Louis for eight years and then went to work in the missions of India. His time there made a profound impression on him. Years later he returned to India to design the chapels in two Marianist houses. On August 6, 2006, in a ceremony marking the end of his Benedictine novitiate, he received his new name, Martin. He is currently a member of the monastic community of Saint Meinrad Archabbey in southern Indiana.

I discovered Martin through is figurative art, but it was not until later that I learned the extent of his talent. He holds a BA in fine arts from the Art Institute of San Antonio, he attended Boston University's master's program in ceramics, and obtained a certificate in liturgical design from the Catholic Theological Union. He had a career working as a designer with Emil Frei glass studio and has designed worship spaces and furniture for numerous churches. He continues to work in all of these mediums and also serves as a cantor.

Brother Martin and I share a love of medieval art. The influence of early mosaics, Byzantine miniatures, Carolignian ivories, Romanesque capitals, sculpture, and glass of the thirteenth century on his work is obvious. The Middle Ages had a passion for order: nothing was left to chance, every action was pre-determined. For example, God the Father, God the Son, the angels, and the apostles are always shown with their feet bare, but it would be improper to represent the Virgin and the saints with bare feet. The gesture of a hand or a finger, the movement of the body, all have meaning. While symbolism continued in art, the Council of Trent marked the end of obeying old artistic traditions and the beginning of exercising artistic license.

The majority of images in this book have appeared on the covers of *Breaking Bread, Today's Missal, Music Issue, Respond & Acclaim* and *Misal del Día*. When asked by OCP's publisher, John Limb, to compile these works into a book, I welcomed the idea. We have added a few other pieces to give you a sense of the diversity of Martin's work.

It is our hope that as you look at and mediate on these images, you will discover the beauty of the symbols, the strength of Martin's art, the richness of the color he uses and his knowledge of theology. As in medieval times, "it was through the medium of art that the highest conceptions of theologians and scholars were passed down to the humblest of people." (Emile Mâle, *The Gothic Image*).

— Jean Germano, OCP Art Director (retired September 2005)

"Good liturgical art is supposed to speak to your soul. Each time you see it, it will engage you and invite you to return again to pray and discover."

Brother Martin Erspamer, OSB

I am grateful to: John Limb, Publisher of OCP, for his vision; Justin DuVall, Archabbot of Saint Meinrad, for his permission to go forward; Father Tobias Colgan, OSB; Father Harry Hagan, OSB; Father Guerric DeBona, OSB; Mary Jeanne Schumacher; John Farless; Bill Sheets; Bari Colombari; Susan Irish, who made it all come together; and Brother Martin, who has enriched my life. *— JG*

FOREWORD

by Archabbot Justin DuVall, OSB
11 July 2007, Solemnity of Saint Benedict

The sound of Gregorian chant evokes a note of transcendence in the contemporary soul, suspending for a while the limits within which the present world confines us. In his *Rule for Monasteries*, however, Saint Benedict paid much more attention to the material things of our daily lives than the present times might suspect of a tradition that has been highly romanticized. Such mundane matters as the proper fit of a habit, the timely harvest of the crops, and the work of any artisans in the monastery, all had a place in the life of the monks who were seeking God before anything else. In the mind of Saint Benedict, material things were quite capable of bearing the weight of glory ascribed to heavenly things.

In the 1,500 years of Benedictine monastic history, the countless, and often nameless, followers of Saint Benedict extended their minds through the development of the arts, both practical and fine. Those arts gave visible expression to the manifold beauty of the imaginations that produced them, and showed how they reflect the mind of the Creator who was honored in their works. At the same time, these religious and artistic men helped preserve and enrich the cultures within which the monasteries flourished, providing an abiding witness to the ability of the human spirit to reach beyond the limits of a given time and place.

The body of work presented in this volume carries on the ancient bloodline of art as experience of the transcendent. While a relatively recent newcomer to the monastery, Brother Martin certainly reflects the soul of a monk in his work. It possesses the power to disclose a truth and a reality beyond itself, a quality which characterizes the Benedictine approach to the material things that fill our lives. The visual arts, no less than chant, can raise our minds and hearts to God, and the hymn of God's praises rises from the works featured in this book.

To all who will take up this volume: look with your soul at the beauty it offers. It gives color and shape and texture to the hope "that in all things God may be glorified" (*Rule of Benedict*, chapter 57: "On the Artisans of the Monastery").

PREFACE

by Guerric DeBona, OSB, Saint Meinrad Archabbey

Contemplation on Glass: The Liturgical Artist And the Re-creation of the Christian Assembly

We first catch sight of God in the Bible as a cosmic craftsman, tearing chaos in half, shaping the edges of the firmament, painting the light in the skies, and finally, breathing life into every living creature. Scripture is filled with the incessant works of the Lord who transforms a people into his own: the rainbow of the covenant, water from the rock in the desert, the Red Sea parted in two. In Psalm 8 the psalmist echoes a refrain that contemplates in ecstatic thanksgiving the spectacular wonders which Almighty God fashioned out of nothing; he marvels at the miracle of creation and the destiny of divine love for humanity: "When I look at your heavens, the work of your fingers, the moon and the stars that you have established; what are human beings that you are mindful of them, mortals that you care for them" (Psalm 8:3-4; NRSV). With the Sermon on the Mount, Jesus teaches his followers not to mind worldly things. Jesus himself says God's ingenious hand cares for all things in love, especially humanity, and advises the disciples "to consider the lilies of the field" which are beyond the pale of the great King Solomon in all his glory. Indeed, Jesus reminds us that creation bears witness to the holy, a sign of God's care for us. Ultimately, the resurrection of Christ from the dead testifies God's eternal fidelity and triumphal creativity over death's destructive, decaying powers. Like a master builder, God never fails to refashion in mercy and love, to recreate us in Christ.

Artists respond in a unique way to the marvels of creation. Those who labor with their hands to bring to light new and original works of art invariably recall God as a creator, a sculptor who fashioned the first human being out of clay. Artists conceive a luminous, dazzling window into the divine. With their unique role in fostering prayer for the Christian community through sacred images and songs of praise, liturgical artists have a crucial place in the Church by engaging and educating the imaginative world of God's people. As Patrick W. Collins wrote, "Surely it is in our imaginations that we are most the *imago Dei*. In those activities of imagining we not only respond to and understand our world, we also share in creating the world. Imagination waits to be turned into creation."[1]

On a steamy July day in Texas in 1971, a gifted, imaginative moment was waiting to unfold. The shadow of a welded steel crucifix, designed and fashioned by the well-known liturgical craftsman Brother Mel Meyer, SM claimed the attention—and the conversion—of a talented young man almost four decades ago in a colorful chapel on the campus of Saint Mary's University in San Antonio, Texas. Brother Martin (Stephen) Erspamer was then a seventeen-year-old nascent Marianist just learning to grasp the fate of his artistic and religious vocation; that calling would absorb the scope of the rest of his life, span the globe and ultimately take him to the contemplative life in a Benedictine monastery in southern Indiana. "I hadn't yet consciously put art and faith together," Erspamer recalls his initial encounter with the striking liturgical environment at Saint Mary's Chapel, "but when I saw this place, and heard the music they composed—this was a place where faith was alive. Not cranking out tunes from a hymnbook but creating it new."[2] Brother Mel's significant influence was a clear inspiration on the young brother, but over the years Brother Martin would evolve his own inventive style. And his liturgical art in painting, glass, furniture and ceramics would draw from "the mystery of redemption a unique power to provoke and invite the world more deeply into the mysteries of our faith."[3]

Born on July 28, 1953 in Iron Mountain, Michigan, into a military family, Brother Martin lived most of his formative years in San Antonio. Having attended a Marianist high school in that city, Erspamer was drawn into the spirituality of the Society of Mary and then towards a career in art. After his religious profession in 1972, he sharpened his craft at Boston University, where he received his MFA. But Brother Martin would face a turning point when his religious sensibilities clashed with the secular world of the haute couture galleries in Boston. He remembers that the curators of the galleries told him that his art work, "smacks of religious symbolism." This encounter was a moment of truth and the birth of a liturgical artist. Already sensitive to the expansive, populist expressions of artistic forms widely available such as murals and folk art in many cultures such as Mexico and South America, Brother Martin would distance himself from the elitist world of the uptown gallery and focus his attention on articulating his own religious idiom. In the meantime, and rather unassumingly, he would silently educate the sacramental imagination of the people of God.

Over the next thirty years, Brother Martin renovated over fifty churches, bringing his democratic sensibilities, stylistic influence, and Catholic liturgical principles to worshipers all across the country. Countless parishes and religious educators have deployed his well known clip art to embellish their own worship aids. His paintings have been reproduced on covers for many OCP missals, which has allowed countless worshipers to expand their own hearts toward the love of God. The recipient of several prestigious awards, including the Modern Liturgy Bene Award and the Helreigel-Burbach Award, Brother Martin has amassed an enormous body of work in various media, all of which share a single common denominator: "that in all things God may be glorified." This lifelong motto, so familiar to the Benedictine way of life, ultimately drew the fifty-year-old Marianist to become a monk himself, moving to Saint Meinrad Archabbey in 2004, where he continues his work in liturgical arts and worship. Brother Martin's prodigious output reminds us of the very purpose of liturgical art and Christian beauty: the proclamation of "something new and original, manifesting itself as an echo of God's own creative act."[4] Coursing through the span of Brother Martin's productive career and enviable artistic development, there are at least three qualities that dominate the body of his work and which I will address briefly here: expressiveness, economy and transcendence.

Even a cursory look at Brother Martin's water color paintings—either as designs for stained glass or as covers for liturgical books—reveals a quality of restrained expressiveness. The figures, like the angels in the stained glass windows commissioned for Immaculate Heart Church in Atlanta, harbor a medieval, iconic *gravitas*. At the same time, though, these representations show us something of an exalted mood in their very bodies, particularly the head, hands and feet. Like the carvings on the great cathedrals in Western Europe, the elongation in the bodily extremities gesture towards a refined, illusive emotion. The wondrously large eyes of the figures even those that remain closed—seem to suggest a contemplative awareness of the Spirit working deep within them. The angels or saints often appear poised between prayerful restraint and something like a genial, emotional longing. They are docile, yet expressively quite vibrant. Furthermore, the accentuated hands are very purposeful, even catechetical, as they are in the depiction of the sower of the seed, a gorgeous window for Saint Joseph Church in Fayette, Missouri. The sower looks across a field like a visionary, and his large hands appear ready to spring forth the Word. Then again, consider the Last Supper that appeared on the cover of *Breaking Bread* 2007. Jesus is at the head of the table prayerfully poised in an *orans* position. Christ's contemplative posture is in sharp contrast to most of the apostles whose facial gestures express a rainbow of emotions, from frank astonishment to prayerful joy. The hands of the apostles silently gesture in a language seemingly all their own and underline the state of their facial features. We can imagine ourselves eavesdropping on this crucial scene in the life of Jesus and the Church. Here, as elsewhere, Brother Martin gleans a great deal of movement from a small, confined space: by depicting the apostles in various emotional registers, the painting imagines the human face around a table from every conceivable angle and reaction. Needless to say, the variety of expressions depicted in the Last Supper plumbs the well of human emotion present in the gathered assembly that remembers the very same eucharistic meal. Good liturgical art enables the congregation to trace their collective autobiography as a people of God in a sacred space.

There is a palpable movement, though carefully reserved, in the way the design and color interacts with light in the abstract stained glass as well. I am thinking here of the way that the classical arches nicely calm the vibrant bolts of ecstatic lines and light in the windows commissioned for the chapel at the Jesuit residence in St. Louis, Missouri. Such movement remains pivotal to liturgical art, lending itself in ecstatic motion to gather the Christian community.

Along with the influences of Western art and architecture, Brother Martin's art reflects some characteristics of the East, as well. Together with abstract representations, many of these figures, saints, angels, apostles and, perhaps most notably, Christ himself, are echoes of the ancient culture of India and Europe.

In 1978, Brother Martin felt called to a Marianist foundation in Bihar, in the northern area of India. His experience in that country was both remarkable and deeply influential. Indian culture is flush with vibrant, astonishing color and ripe with the same sinuous limbs that also find themselves in Brother Martin's art. Like the "Dancing Shiva," with its dynamic, triumphal, and elastic body gestures, Brother Martin's art often penetrates the confines of space which, interestingly, appears to contain that very motion: the Christ at table, the Christ on the cross, the Christ in glory, sharing his very life with his disciples. As the design never seems limited to its own space, a real sense of freedom emerges in these pieces. Even the abstract patterns extend our attention to God's work in human history: the active movement of grace, alive and shimmering in the world, waiting to be named. Finally, Brother Martin's expressive representations of figures on glass and popular worship books highlight the important liturgical gestures of the Christian assembly: the hands for offering gifts, the eyes to be opened and the feet to be washed.

Secondly, an economy of line and space characterizes Brother Martin's art as well. It is well known that liturgical art is not a focal point in itself, but meant to serve

Christian worship. *Built of Living Stones* reminds us that "artworks truly belongs in the church when they are worthy of the place of worship and when they enhance the liturgical, devotional, and contemplative prayer they are inspired to serve."[5] This observation suggests a certain simplicity to the artifacts that fill the worship space, perhaps best encountered in Brother Martin's design for liturgical furniture. The ambo, for instance, at Immaculate Heart of Mary in New Melle, Missouri, is not only clean and lean in its minimalist design, but the Church's Lectionary itself rests on a large open space, bridging two supports. The design for the ambo represents an extreme departure from the ornate pre-Conciliar pulpits of Western Europe. It is striking that the open space seems to suggest that the word of God stands on its own, awaiting proclamation. Moreover, the body of the one who proclaims and preaches is clearly visible, filling the void, as it were, and partnering him or her in the word. Similarly, the narthex table for the same church is also supported by a clean design. Open windows are cast in steel at the center, lending both an openness and a familiarity to the piece. The community of faith is invited to place its symbols of welcome and remembrance on the table, making it a particularly inviting and practical piece for many purposes.

I find the altar for Immaculate Heart of Mary one of Brother Martin's most arresting liturgical pieces. The extraordinarily large piece of red granite is noticeably separate from the body of the altar, which is clean and substantial. In keeping with the revised *Rite of Dedication of a Church and Altar*, Brother Martin has positioned a lovely oak and walnut reliquary beneath it. The reliquary, highlighted with gold leaf, can be viewed by the assembly as a reminder that the Church is literally built on the bones of the blessed. Although the reliquary itself takes a rather traditional shape for the keeping of relics, it looks something like a small church, a house for the saints. Brother Martin reminds the assembly that the altar is unlike any other church furnishing: the symbol of Christ the anointed of God, the altar remains the focal point and the symbolic gathering point for the Christian assembly.

Brother Martin's intuitive sense of artistic economy finds itself in other media as well. When speaking of his work in ceramics, for instance, Brother Martin says he conceives of an object in clay "not unlike a figure—with a foot, a belly and a lip,"—all of which have an organic relationship to the whole. There is never anything excessive in any of his work, and he consciously strives to get the creations to their essence; in the case of the figures, to lay bare their most hidden passions and contemplative desires. Brother Martin clearly has a modernist sensibility, but he views his stylistic temperament as something like artistic common sense. "All art relies on the same rules of good design and composition," he once told me. When it comes to economy, that artistic discipline is particularly evident in the way in which narration has been conflated in both paintings and stained glass. Consider, for instance, the Saint Meinrad triptych, commissioned as a shrine for the renovation of the Church of Maria Einsiedeln at Saint Meinrad Archabbey. The choice of a triptych allowed Brother Martin to collapse several stories into a single composition, which details the life of Saint Meinrad and the history of Saint Meinrad Archabbey and Abbey church. There are several stories coursing through the triptych, replete with representations from the life of Saint Meinrad, hermit and martyr, portraits of the founders of the Abbey from the motherhouse of Einsiedeln in Switzerland, together with abbots who built and then renovated the church. Despite the multiplication of stories and the collapsing of narrative time, there is a fine unity of composition, along with a sense of balance and well-chosen color throughout. Saint Meinrad and the other monks harbor similar features, suggesting that all those who follow the Rule of Saint Benedict are called to emulate the saints. The piece is elegantly poised and full of narrative motion.

In using a triptych to tell a story, Brother Martin has recalled a legacy of Christian art to serve the contemporary Church. Several histories are often entwined in a triptych, an art form that has its origins in the Byzantine Empire of Christian antiquity and later became very typical as narrational vehicles for shrines in Gothic churches. Such panels allowed an enormous amount of information to be conflated in a relatively small space.

Brother Martin can trace his feel for economy to one of his visits to the Basilica of Saint Magdalene of the Abbey of Vézelay in France. The sculpted scene over the main entrance is typical of the medieval sanctified world view: all creation bends into harmony within a divine frame. It is God the Artist who conceives the workings of the universe in perfect harmony; all things are subsumed into the mysterious workings of the Divine Will and into the spectrum of Christ himself, the Alpha and the Omega. For the renovation of Saint Joseph Church in Fayette, Missouri, Brother Martin created a series of windows detailing the parables of Jesus on one side of the nave, while on the other side he depicted the days of creation. In these double windows, we can sense a narrative economy issuing from salvation history: the Lord God created the heavens and the earth, while the Son recreates and redeems by sowing the word. The assembly stands in the center of both as sanctified beneficiaries of the word made visible.

Brother Martin's art suggests that a greater reality is at stake, and this quality discloses a third characteristic, a transcendent world that is hard to miss in his liturgical expressions. The vocation of the artist quietly invites the human family into a world not their own by confronting the imagination with graced possibility. Karl Rahner put it this way: "Of their very nature artists are discoverers of a concrete situation in which persons concretely realize their transcendental being in a new way, one that differs from former ways."[6] Authentic art converts us and compels us to look both through and, yes, beyond our own horizon. The liturgical artist draws us ever deeper into the mystery of the infinite precisely through the finite materials of the artifacts themselves. *Built of Living Stones* insists that the quality of a work of art mirrors the Creator and that "the integrity and energy of a piece of art, produced individually by the labor of an artist, is always to be preferred above objects that are mass-produced," and that "designs that are of short-lived popularity are unworthy."[7] Liturgical pieces ought to echo an enduring tradition that speaks not of fads but an eternal verity. That transcendent state is suggested by the choice of materials and in the design of Brother Martin's liturgical furnishings. His altars, ambos, presidential chairs and tabernacles are composed of authentic materials; these are gleaned from the natural universe that has been entrusted to the people of God for their use, not recycled objects that are ready to be disposed of and quickly forgotten. With clean designs, the furniture exposes the simple, natural state of creation from which they were taken.

Brother Martin evokes an inspirational, awe-inspiring quality in his representations of religious figures as well, typically through his use of color. When we glimpse at his stained glass figures penetrated by a glorious orchestra of light and color that imagines them emanating from a source beyond themselves, these creations proclaim what is everlasting and holy. The spectacular use of luminous color allows for a mystical mood in worship that is there to transform, to recall the rainbow of the covenant, and not simply to be consumed as an art object. The vibrant and lavish aura of the spectrum of blues that surround Christ create a calming effect, while the bold red suggests passion, sacrifice, and authority. Deep crimsons and marine colors proclaim the crucifixion scene in Immaculate Heart of Mary in New Melle, Missouri, against a background of earth tones and grays in glass. Framed by natural oak, the crucified Christ surely stands out in bold relief as the singularly most important event in the history of humankind. It is as if the entire composition of wood, glass and color are bowing to the solemn occasion of Christ's salvific death for all. Situated behind the altar, the crucifix is also used as a processional cross, brought to the congregation as the Great Standard before the congregation, further accentuating the exalted status of that enduring symbol. The relationship between the lush reds and blues over and against the more muted colors suggest a contrast that I believe is present in Brother Martin's work overall and helps to further accentuate the quality of the transcendent. Indeed Brother Martin achieves a fine tension between economy of line on the one hand and a dazzling use of color on the other in many of his paintings and windows. The figures themselves are often boldly defined and even shy in their simplicity, while the color is quite electric in its vibrancy. Astonishing color then gifts the assembly with the new, unexpected, and re-creative in Christian worship.

The transcendent quality in Brother Martin's art serves not to evoke a utopia, but to inspire a human longing for God, who dwells in unapproachable light. I read the figures on glass and paper as individuals captured in a moment of grace, a sharing in the unfolding of God's love and mercy. Brother Martin has depicted stories from salvation history in various media that remind us of our connection with the larger story which God himself, the Author of Life, is writing. While postmodern culture faces the potential loss of a "metanarrative," or the bankruptcy of a larger human story into which it may be gathered, Brother Martin's liturgical art reminds the Christian community of salvation history and the wonderful works God has done. Those who have come from the margins of a fragmented society are gathered together in an ecclesial space bright with festivals of song, an astonishing continuum of light, and a banquet of sacred memory to accompany the community of the blessed. The figures that have been gleaned from the Scriptures and tradition now find new life as they embellish windows, shrines, and the pages of liturgical books; they are saints like Francis, Juan Diego, Patrick and King David, not aloof and distant, but made present and vital in the Catholic imagination. Remembering the saints as those who have gone before us marked with the sign of faith helps to satisfy what Redemptorist James Wallace has named "our hunger for belonging."[8] Good liturgical art which imagines a space for those who are blessed in the Christian story inspires the community to think and feel and believe beyond itself. Appropriately enough, Brother Martin's liturgical representations are not distant memories of historical figures, but familiar friends, the blessed who are welcomed by those gathered to pray. The community of faith traces its graced history in the company of the saints.

Ultimately, the transcendent in Brother Martin's art reveals the God who is both beyond and before us: all holy mystery and yet mysteriously present in the community of love. Brother Martin has placed his art in the hands of the gathered assembly so that all creation may give thanks and praise together in one voice. In the end, his art points us back to the liturgy, which is the work of the people of God offered to give thanks and praise to the Father of all blessings. Taken together and viewed as a whole, which this volume intends to offer, we discover in Brother Martin's prayerful and imaginative work the very purpose of liturgical art: to lead the Christian community into God's inexpressible love—a love that, in Saint Benedict's words, casts out fear.

---

[1] Patrick W. Collins, "Spirituality, the Imagination and the Arts," *Ars Liturgiae Worship, Aesthetics and Praxis: Essays in Honor of Nathan D. Mitchell*, edited by Claire V. Johnson (Chicago: Liturgy Training Publications, 2003), 147-48.

[2] Jeannette Batz, "The Artist's Way: The Spiritual Path of a Marianist Artist," *National Catholic Reporter.*

[3] USCCB, *Built of Living Stones: Art, Architecture and Worship* (Washington, D.C.: USCCB, 2002), 50.

[4] *Living Stones*, 50

[5] *Living Stones*, 50

[6] Karl Rahner, "Art Against the Horizon of Theology and Piety," *Theological Investigations, XXIII: Final Writings*, translated by Joseph Donceel, S.J. and Hugh M. Riley. (New York: Crossroad, 1992), 166.

[7] *Living Stones*, 51; 55.

[8] James Wallace, CSsR, *Preaching to the Hungers of the Heart: The Homily on the Feasts and Within the Rites* (Collegeville, MN: Liturgical Press, 2002), 109-174.

ART

Drawing is a meditation on simplicity and good design. Taking inspiration from the arts of Christianity of the past, I want to draw in a way that recognizes the centuries of our tradition – the flatness of icon painting, the bold color and strong composition of the Romanesque, the serenity and elegance of the Gothic. It takes years of practice to pare a drawing down to its strong essence. I'm still practicing!

The Shrine of Saint Meinrad

The Shrine of Saint Meinrad sits in the north niche of the Church of Maria Einsiedeln in St. Meinrad, Indiana, and was commissioned for the renovation of that church in 1997. The triptych is seven feet tall and constructed of oak, walnut and purple heart woods. The square side panels to the right depict the life and death of Saint Meinrad; those on the left show the saint in various stages of his life in community and then as a hermit. The right corner of the triptych shows the two founding monks of Saint Meinrad Archabbey from the Abbey of Einsiedeln, Switzerland, while the top left corner portrays the three abbots responsible for the construction and renovation of the present Abbey Church of Saint Meinrad. The lower central panel houses a relic of the martyr Saint Meinrad, hermit and monk. Above the relic, the large central panel depicts an episode in the life of the ninth century monk from the Abbey of Reichenau, Meinrad, who expresses his desire to serve God as a hermit in the Dark Forest to a local woman, who, together with others, provided him with food. His hermitage and the two ravens associated with his life are also included in the scene.

BELOVED MEINRAD MARTYR

Meinrad is invested
in the monastic habit
by the abbot.

Meinrad is a teacher
of the younger monks
in the community.

Meinrad digs the
foundation for his
hermitage in the forest.

Meinrad offers Mass and extends hospitality to a pair of bandits. His pet ravens and the chickens try to warn him.

The thieves beat Meinrad to death and the ravens pursue the thieves.

Monks come to retrieve the remains of Meinrad.

Crucifixion

watercolor, gouache and transparent inks on paper

In many medieval manuscripts and stained glass windows the cross of Jesus was colored green, the color of life. In this image, the body of Jesus is green and from his side comes his blood, which also gives life. The sun and moon, traditional elements in earlier portrayals of the crucifixion, are cosmic witnesses to this momentous event.

Last Supper

watercolor, gouache and transparent inks on paper

This piece was inspired by the lintel stone of the church at Neuillyen-Donjon. The composition was originally a single row of figures arranged horizontally. In order to fit the missal cover, the figures were repositioned to work vertically.

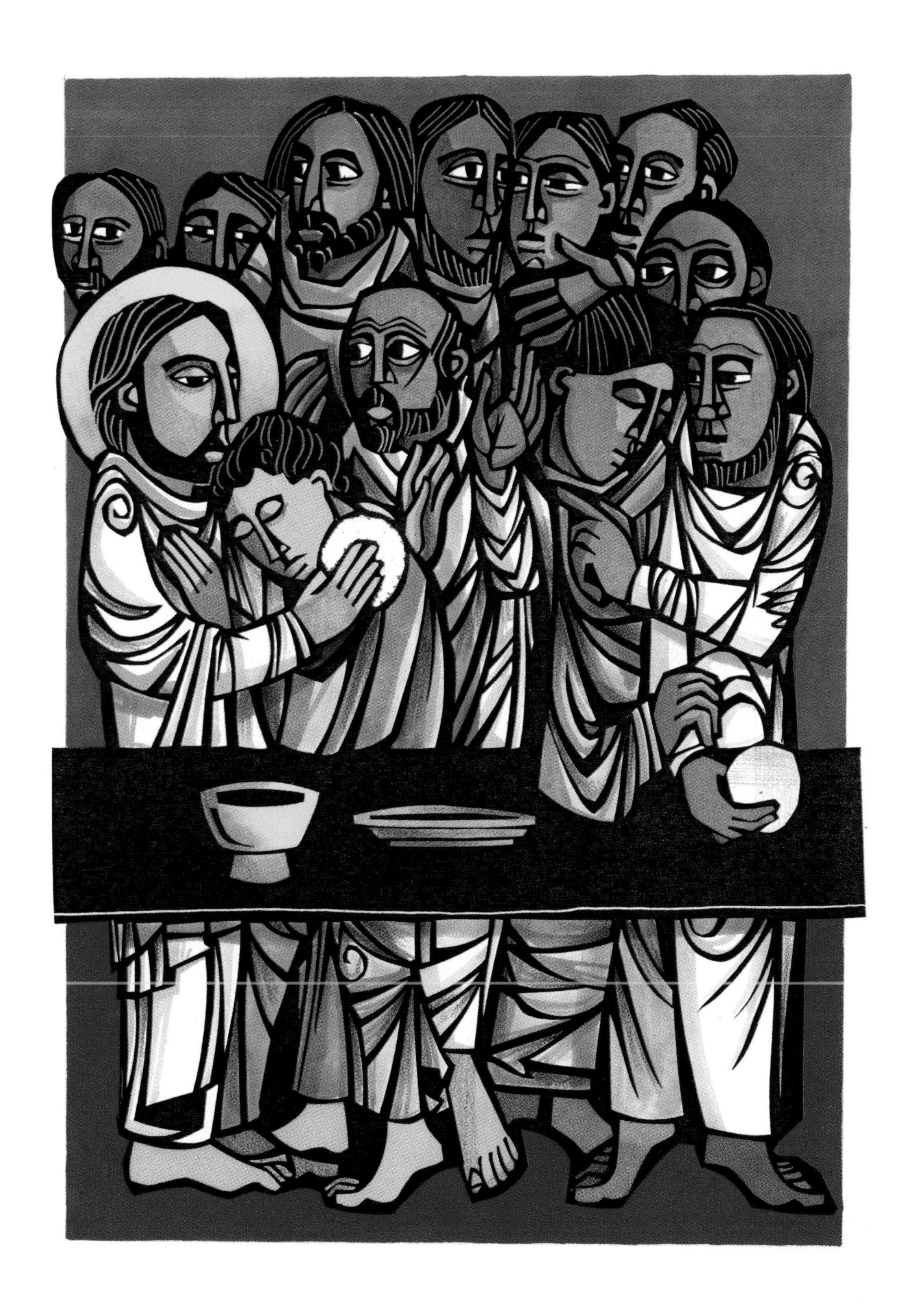

The Transfiguration

watercolor, gouache and transparent inks on paper

This is a more contemporary version of this subject based on a variety of manuscript paintings. The position of the apostles' hands signify wonder and a degree of fear and bewilderment. In the original paintings, the apostles have fallen to the ground and are covering their faces and heads.

Juan Diego Displays the Tilma

hand-cut amberlith film in color-separated plates

I am very fond of woodcuts and linocuts. The amberlith cut with a razor gives the same kind of sharp cut line as does a woodcut tool on a block. This piece was made for the cover of a book published by St. Anthony Messenger Press.

The Wedding Feast of Cana

watercolor, gouache and transparent inks on paper

In 2005, shortly before entering the monastery, I took a last trip to France and Germany to see a few of my favorite places again. Driving toward Bourges, I came upon the small church at Brinay sur Cher. The interior is covered with twelfth century frescoes. This composition was inspired by the fresco of the same theme.

Christus Victor Rex

watercolor, gouache and transparent inks on paper

This piece was inspired by an Ottonian ivory carving. The figure of Christ had an interesting almond-shaped face that I liked.

previous spread

Musicians and Miriam Dancing

watercolor, gouache and transparent ink on paper

This piece was intended as a wrap-around cover for an OCP missal. Miriam dances at the Hebrews' deliverance from the pharaoh's armies. Sometimes I think it is a good idea to feature the feminine heroes in our faith history as well as the men.

facing page

The Multiplication of the Loaves and Fishes

hand-cut amberlith film

Christ's position as he blesses the basket of fish was taken from a medieval Spanish reliquary carved in ivory.

The Nativity

watercolor, gouache and transparent inks on paper

Working with stained glass has made me a little more adventuresome when choosing color in painting. The German Expressionist painters, especially Emile Nolde, are much admired by me because of their use of strong color.

Christ in Majesty

watercolor, gouache and transparent inks on paper

Over the years, I have done many versions of this seated Christ figure. He is enthroned as Lord of Creation, seated on an abstraction of the rainbow with the earth as his footstool. He sits within the almond-shaped halo, the mandorla, formed by the overlapping of two circles that are themselves symbols of infinity. The sun and the moon witness his majesty. The Greek letters stand for "Jesus Christ, victor ."

IC XC
NI KA

The Last Supper

watercolor, gouache and transparent inks on paper

This composition tries to capture some of the emotional agitation or turmoil going on in the hearts of the apostles during this meal.

The Adoration of the Magi

watercolor, gouache and transparent ink on paper

Inspired by a medieval English window, the figure of the child Jesus looks older than he is. In many pieces from this time, the Christ child often looks like a miniature adult. I have tried to reflect that here.

The Jesse Tree

watercolor, gouache and transparent inks on paper

This composition, which appeared first at Abbot Suger's Saint Denis and shortly after at Chartres has always been fascinating to me. Jesse, the father of King David, is asleep at the bottom of the composition. A tree grows from his loins, symbolizing the royal lineage of Jesus. It is a medieval construction of some earthiness and shows a true appreciation for the means by which the incarnation became a reality.

Towards Bethlehem

watercolor, gouache and transparent inks on paper

The pregnant Mary sits atop the donkey on her journey to Bethlehem with Joseph. The donkeys in this type of scene carved on pillar capitals have often given me much delight. The anonymous artists responsible for them seem to have caught the true essence of the donkey. This image pays homage to them.

King David Plays the Harp

watercolor, gouache and transparent inks on paper

Manuscript paintings were very structured, but one of the enjoyable things about many of these compositions is the way the figures within them break out of the frame in places, giving the art a freshness.

previous spread

Make a Joyful Noise to the Lord

watercolor, gouache and transparent inks on paper

This is another wrap-around composition created for an OCP missal cover. I was particularly happy with the strong color in this piece. Often people ask me why the figures have shoes that are two different colors. It's not symbolic of anything; it is just a way to introduce a spark of color into another area of the painting.

facing page

King David Plays the Harp

watercolor, gouache and transparent inks on paper

In my travels throughout France and Germany looking for Romanesque and Gothic churches, especially those with glass preserved from those periods, I have come to greatly admire the work of generations of anonymous craftsmen and glass painters. Their work shows a confidence with a brush that is second to none. The sinuous lines painted into the drapery of figures is particularly wonderful. Areas of concentric curves or parallel lines alternate with expanses of unpainted glass. This technique gives a dynamism to the figures.

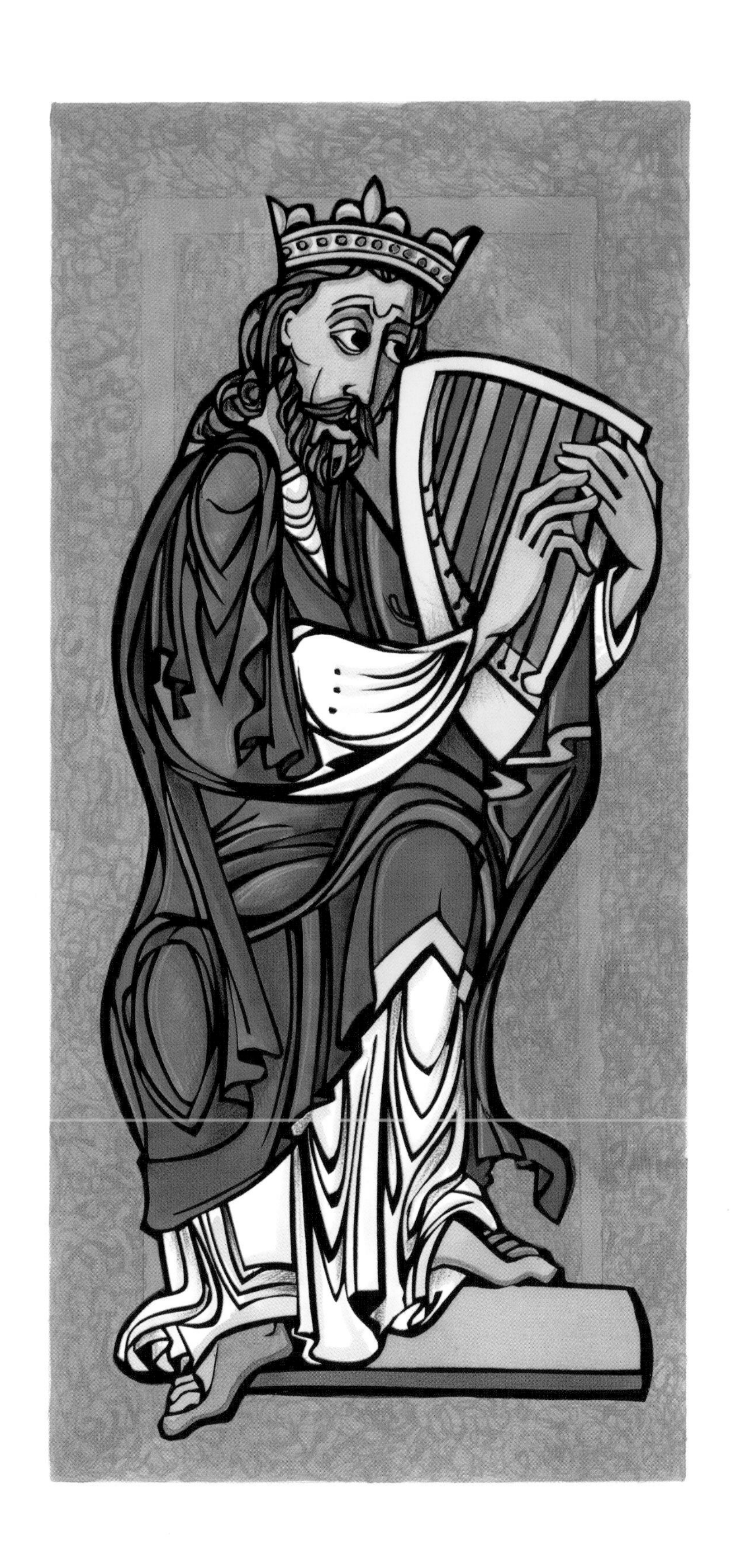

Seated Figure of Christ

watercolor, gouache and transparent inks on paper

This was a companion piece for the King David figure on page 55.

Emmaus

watercolor, gouache and transparent inks on paper

Alternating between working in stained glass and illustration is good, I think. The influences of one technique begin to make themselves known in the other medium. This illustration is a clear example of when that happens: the blue panel behind the head of Christ was something I was also playing with in a window design at the time.

Saint Patrick

hand-cut amberlith film with two color-separated plates

When I first started sending in illustrations done with this technique, Jean Germano called me and said the graphic designers remarked, "Oh, so this is amberlith. We heard about this in the History of Graphics class." Saint Patrick holds his traditional attribute, the three-leaf clover, symbol of the Trinity.

The Cross, The Tree of Life

watercolor, gouache and transparent inks on paper

On page 26 in this book, the symbol of the green cross was discussed. Another prevalent image in this symbolic language was that the wood of Jesus' cross was actually taken from the Tree of the Knowledge of Good and Evil. The tree that brought death to the human race through the sin of Adam was the very same tree that brought us back to life through the sacrifice of Jesus, the New Adam.

LOAVES AND FISHES

watercolor, gouache and transparent inks on paper

This image was inspired by an early Christian mosaic floor in the Holy Land.

facing page

THE ANGEL AT THE TOMB

watercolor, gouache and transparent inks on paper

This composition was originally vertically oriented and included the soldiers sleeping beneath the angel on the tomb. The soldiers were removed from the illustration to fit the missal cover.

·WHY DO YOU LOOK FOR THE LIVING AMONG THE DEAD?·

The Feeding of the Multitude

watercolor, gouache and transparent inks on paper

This piece was painted at a time when both illustration and stained glass design were being created during the same weeks. The influence of stained glass is very strong in this painting.

Christ Enthroned with Saints

watercolor, gouache and transparent inks on paper

The figure of Christ in this piece was influenced by a Romanesque German missal cover done in ivory.

Christ and Ecclesia

watercolor, gouache and transparent inks on paper

This crucifixion composition contains the additional figure of a crowned woman, the figure of Ecclesia, the Church. Christ is portrayed as the New Adam Just as Eve came forth from the side of Adam in Genesis, so the Church came forth from the blood of Christ, the New Adam.

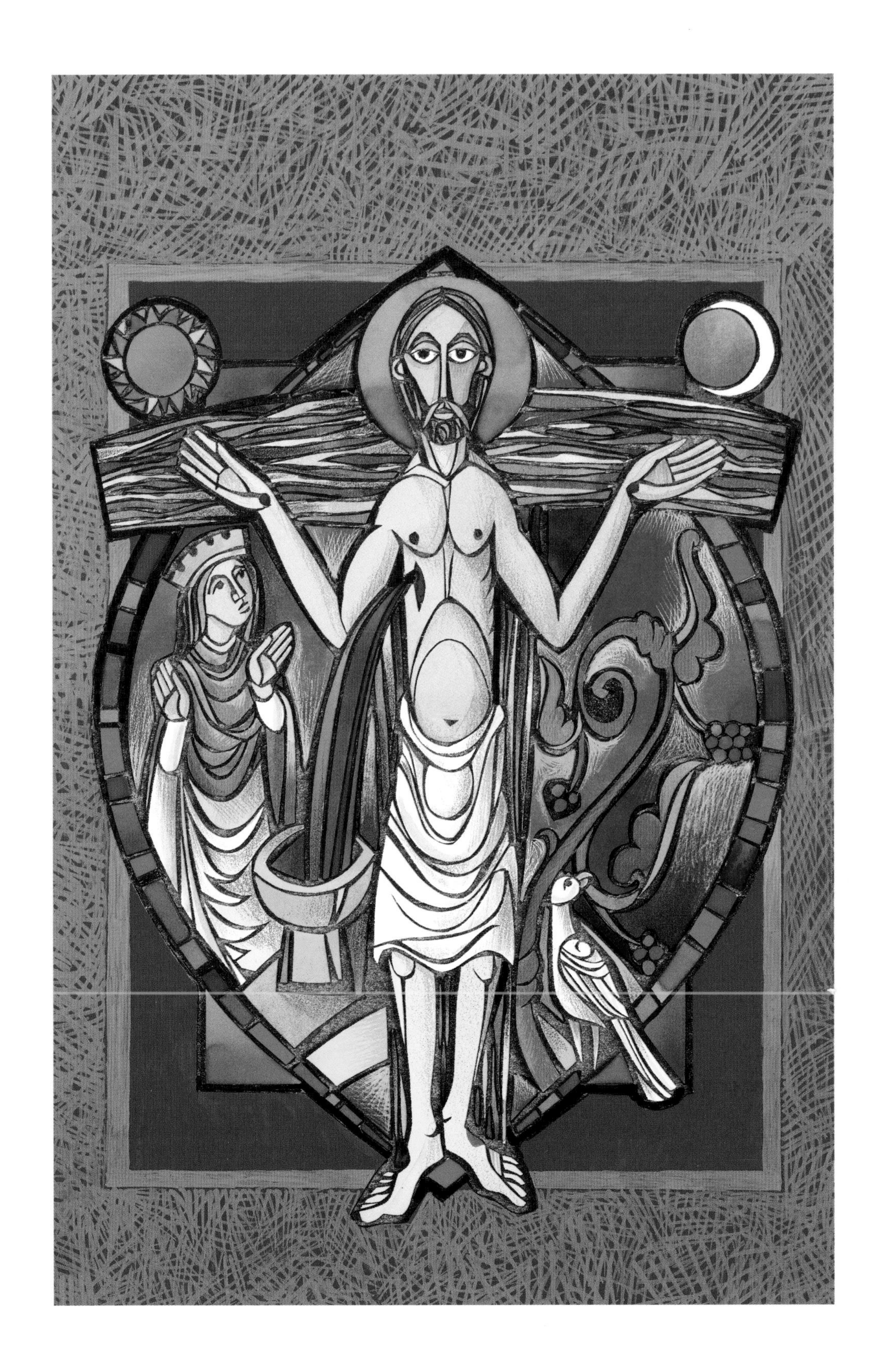

Saint Francis and the Birds

scratchboard

Saint Francis is rendered in a black figure with white line technique, common in woodcuts and linocuts. This figure was influenced by the work of Eric Gill, typographer and artist of the English arts and crafts movement.

The Crucifixion

watercolor, gouache and transparent inks on paper

This painting is one of a new series of works begun since my arrival at the monastery. It is looser and more stylized than previous works. It represents a direction I would like to pursue. This piece was painted as an illustration for the cover of a book written by a number of monks here in the monastery.

GLASS

Stained glass is a wonderful medium I have been blessed to work with over many years. The material itself is lovely – its crystalline brilliance and its textural qualities: bubbly, striated, opalescent, or combed and wavy. Each texture refracts the light in a different way. Abbot Suger of Saint Denis was right: when contemplating the light of heaven that filters through a window's jeweled tones, one is transported to a different reality. The heavenly Jerusalem seems very near indeed.

The Parable of the Sower and the Seed

leaded mouth-blown glass, metallic oxides, and diamond drilling

This is a detail of one window from a large series of windows in the Church of Saint Joseph in Fayette, Missouri. The windows on one side of the nave depict the days of creation. On the other side of the nave, the windows present the parables and stories of Jesus. The rich, jewel-tone color is especially pleasing to me.

previous spread

Windows: Chapel of Saint Ignatius of Loyola

mouthblown leaded crystal, metallic oxides

There are nine windows in this chapel inspired by the writings of Jesuit Teilhard de Chardin. The windows have no painted oxides on them, allowing the architecture of the neighborhood to interact with the textures in the glass. This chapel is on the eighteenth floor of a building in downtown St. Louis and has a breathtaking view of the surrounding area. The Chapel of Saint Ignatius of Loyola is in the Jesuit Community Hall of St. Louis University, St. Louis, Missouri.

facing page

Angel with Trumpet

leaded mouth-blown glass, with metallic oxides

This is a copy of a window that was part of a series of seven windows for Saint Timothy Episcopal Church in St. Louis. The entire series represented the seasons of the liturgical year. I liked this composition so much, that I made a duplicate panel for my own studio here at Saint Meinrad Archabbey.

CERAMICS

The medium I first fell in love with as an artist was clay, and it continues to be one I return to time and time again. It is soft, supple, yielding and seductive. A good glaze can be like skin, subtly revealing the underlying structure. There is a certain familiar comfort in handling a favorite cup or bowl or mug – the fingers search out the way a glaze puddles in one place or how the form bulges or sways in another.

Dough Bowl

earthenware, white slip, Persian turquoise glaze, 20 inch diameter

Chalice and Paten

stoneware, white slip, soda-vapor glaze, 8 inch height

Chalice and Paten

earthenware, terra sigillata, colored slips, matte black glaze and clear glaze, carved and sgrafitto decoration

facing page

Crucifixion

earthenware plate, terra sigillata, matte black glaze, carved and sgrafitto decoration, 30 inch diameter

This piece was made near the end of my time in Boston for graduate school and was part of a show at the Westminster Gallery on Newbury Street.

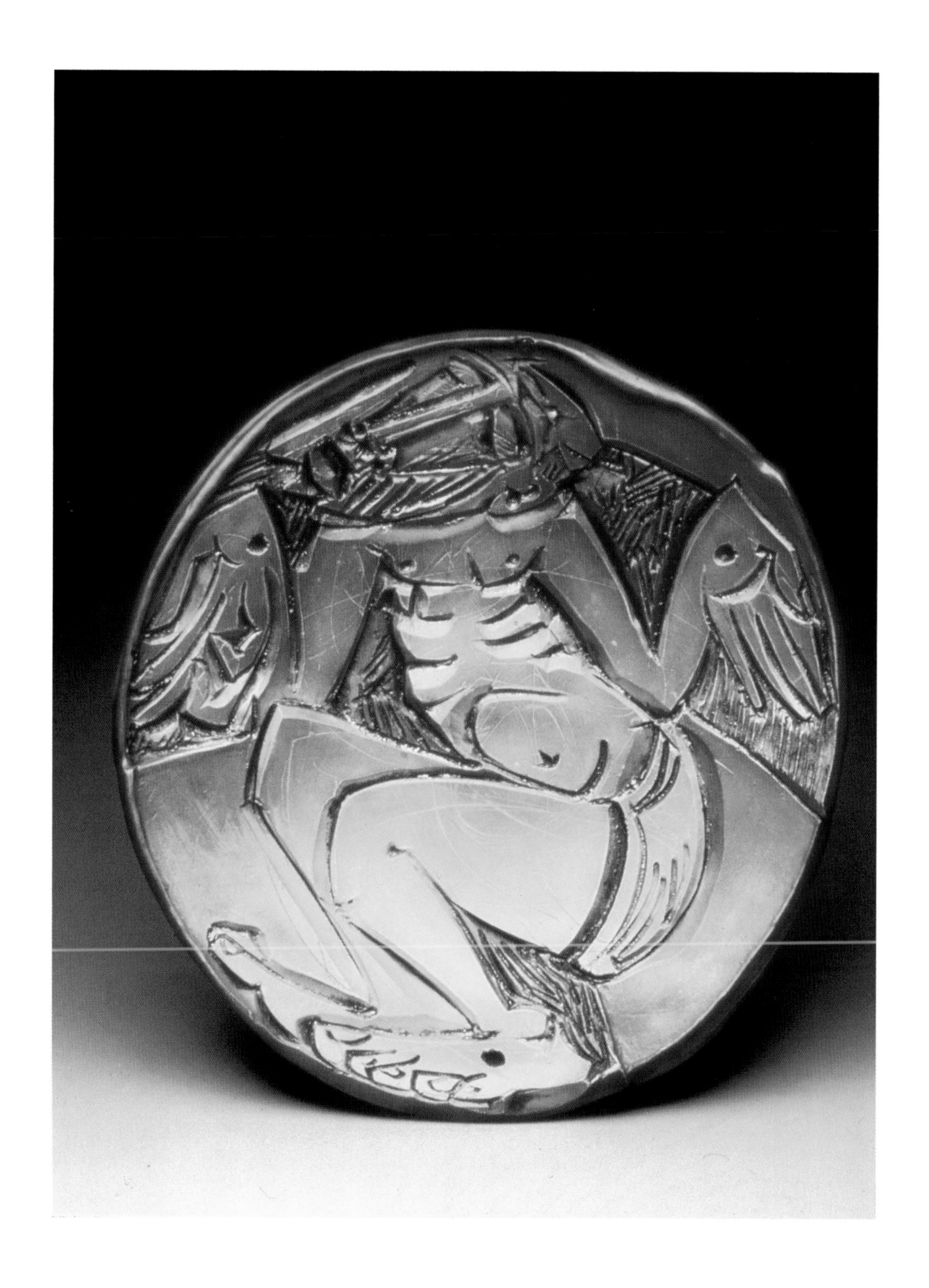

FURNITURE

When designing furniture for liturgical use, I prefer to use good quality but ordinary materials for their fabrication, wood, iron, bronze, dressed but unpolished stone. If the materials are good and the design is good, then these humble materials are transfigured for God's service. They quietly proclaim the greatness and goodness of God's creation.

Ambo

red oak and black walnut

This ambo was designed as part of the sanctuary ensemble for Immaculate Heart of Mary Church in New Melle, Missouri. It is wheelchair accessible. The height of the reading stand can be adjusted to the height of the reader.

All Saints Reliquary

bronze and bonded bronze panels on a wooden carcass, 6 feet in length

This is one of two pieces commissioned by Saint Meinrad Archabbey for the renovation of its church completed in 1997. This piece houses part of the monastery's substantial collection of relics. Monks profess their vows in the presence of relics and, at Saint Meinrad, deceased monks are waked in front of this shrine.

Processional Cross

wood panel, gesso and acrylic pigments painted in egg tempera style

When the Church of the Immaculate Heart of Mary in New Melle, Missouri, was built a few years ago, the community asked for a processional cross of significant scale to serve as the altar cross. I designed a contemporary version of the early painted crosses. The figures beneath the cross hold bandoliers with an adapted text taken from a monastic processional hymn for the Vespers of Easter.

SUN OF JUSTICE, GIVER OF LIFE
FOUNTAIN OF GRACE, HAIL

RÉSUMÉ

EDUCATION

1997	Certification from the Institute of Liturgical Consultants, Catholic Theological Union (Chicago, Illinois)
1995–97	Post-graduate studies, Catholic Theological Union (Chicago, Illinois)
1986	MFA, Boston University (Boston, Massachusetts)
1976	BFA, St. Mary's University and the Art Institute of San Antonio (San Antonio, Texas)

RELATED EXPERIENCE

2005	Entered Saint Meinrad Archabbey [Benedictine monastery] (St. Meinrad, Indiana)
1987	Summer instructor for graduate program of School for American Craftsmen, Rochester Institute of Technology (Rochester, New York)
1986–07	Illustrator, Liturgy Training Publications (Chicago, Illinois), OCP (Portland, Oregon), St. Anthony Messenger Press (Cincinnati, Ohio)
1986	Dolle lecturer, Saint Meinrad School of Theology (St. Meinrad, Indiana)
1986	Visiting artist at San Antonio Art Institute (San Antonio, Texas), Southern Illinois University (Edwardsville, Illinois), Webster University (St. Louis, Missouri), Maryville University (St. Louis, Missouri)
1985–07	Designer and painter, Emil Frei and Associates Stained Glass, Inc. (St. Louis, Missouri)
1984	Teaching assistant, Boston University (Boston, Massachusetts)
1980	Appointment to Lalit Kala Akademi Studios, sponsored by the Indian Government (New Delhi, India)
1979	Travel throughout Europe and Asia
1971	Entered Society of Mary (the Marianists)

CURRENT LITURGICAL CONSULTATIONS

Assumption of the Blessed Virgin Church (O'Fallon, Missouri)

Christ the Redeemer Church (Atlanta, Georgia)

Immaculate Heart of Mary Church (Atlanta, Georgia)

Immaculate Heart of Mary Church (New Melle, Missouri)

Saint Lawrence Church (Atlanta, Georgia)

Saint Timothy Episcopal Church (St. Louis, Missouri)

RECENT WORKS

2006	Design of windows and appointments for Saint Patrick of Merna Church (Bloomington, Illinois)
2005	Design of interior appointments for Assumption of the Blessed Virgin Church (O'Fallon, Missouri)
2004	Design of interior appointments for Our Lady of Lourdes Church (Washington, Missouri)
2004	Renovation of Epiphany of Our Lord Catholic Church (St. Louis, Missouri)
2000	Design and execution of liturgical space for the North American Academy of Liturgy, National Assembly (St. Louis, Missouri)
2000	Design for stained-glass sanctuary windows for Saint John Neumann Church (St. Charles, Illinois)
2000	Design for renovation of the Marianist Seminary Chapel (Rome, Italy)
2000	Design for stained glass and appointments for Emory University Newman Chapel (Atlanta, Georgia)
2000	Design for renovation, floorplan and appointments of Curia Marianisti/Chiesa Santa Catherina (Rome, Italy)
2000	Design for renovation of Motherhouse Chapel, School Sisters of Notre Dame (St. Louis, Missouri)
2000	Design for renovation of Saint Cletus Church (St. Charles, Missouri)
2000	Design and execution for liturgical space (including large-scale 25 foot x 25 foot painting) for Evangelical Lutheran Church of America, National Assembly, Navy Pier (Chicago, Illinois)
2000	Design of faceted stained-glass windows for Immaculate Conception Church (Dardenne, Missouri)
2000	Sanctuary stained glass for Parkway United Church of Christ (St. Louis, Missouri)
2000	Design for renovation, stained glass, liturgical appointments, floorplan for Christ Prince of Peace Church (St. Louis, Missouri)
1999	Stained-glass sanctuary windows for United Church of Christ (Staunton, Illinois)
1999	Design for stained glass for University of Illinois Newman Center (Charleston, Illinois)
1998	Design of the chapel, The Sarah Community at DePaul Hospital (St. Louis, Missouri)
1998	Design of twenty-four stained-glass windows with Old Testament scenes for Brookings Park Chapel (St. Louis, Missouri)
1998	Commission of reliquary for Marmion Abbey (Joliet, Illinois)
1998	Processional cross for Delbarton Abbey (Delbarton, New Jersey)
1998	Interior design and execution of appointments and glass for Good Shepherd Lutheran Church (Collinsville, Illinois)

1998	Renovation of sanctuary for Saint Mary Church (Trenton, Illinois)
1998	Design of windows and interior for Saint Joseph Church (Cottleville, Missouri)
1998	Design of interior and appointments for Saint Patrick Cathedral (Billings, Montana)
1996	Appointments and design for the chapel for Mother of Perpetual Help Home (St. Louis, Missouri)
1996	Design of monumental-sized banners for Saint Joseph Cathedral (Columbus, Ohio)
1996	Processional cross and candlesticks for Epiphany Church, (St. Louis, Missouri)
1996	Processional cross and candlesticks for Saint Francis de Sales Church (Muskegon, Michigan)
1996	Stained-glass windows for Woodlawn Chapel Presbyterian Church (St. Louis, Missouri)
1995	Processional cross for Saint Justin Martyr Church (St. Louis, Missouri)
1995	Interior of chapel, works in wood, metal, fresco, and stained glass for Holy Rosary Health Center (Miles City, Montana)
1995	Design of monumental-sized wall hangings for Saint Gabriel the Archangel Church (Fayetteville, Georgia)
1993	Design of monumental-sized wall hangings for Saint Justin Martyr Church (St. Louis, Missouri)
1993	Interior of chapel, works in wood, metal, fresco, and stained glass for Spohn Hospital South (Corpus Christi, Texas)
1993	Liturgical setting, works in wood, metal, ceramic, and fabric for the National Association of Pastoral Musicians Convention (St. Louis, Missouri)
1992	Renovation of baptistry for Saint Blaise Church (St. Louis, Missouri)
1990	Interior, works in wood, stone, metal, fresco, ceramic, and stained glass for Our Lady of Guadalupe Church (Helotes, Texas)
1990	Carved stone table for Dr. Susan Pittman (St. Louis, Missouri)
1989	Carved stone baptismal font for Saint Monica Church (St. Louis, Missouri)
1987	Three figures in cast stone for Bethany Lutheran Church (Indianapolis, Indiana)
1982	Chapel interior for Saint Mary High School (Colorado Springs, Colorado)
1982	Fresco mural for Saint Mary High School (Colorado Springs, Colorado)

INDEX OF PLATES